Kyivsky Waltz | Київський Вальс
a love story | історія кохання

poems and art by

KS Lack | КШ Лек

Finishing Line Press
Georgetown, Kentucky

Kyivsky Waltz | Київський Вальс
a love story | історія кохання

Copyright © 2024 by KS Lack
ISBN 979-8-88838-468-8 First Edition
All rights reserved under International and Pan-American Copyright Conventions. No part of this book may be reproduced in any manner whatsoever without written permission from the publisher, except in the case of brief quotations embodied in critical articles and reviews.

ACKNOWLEDGMENTS

"Chkalova Street" was a finalist for the 2022 *Inverted Syntax Sublingua Prize for Poetry* and was published in Issue 4 of the journal.

"Notes from a Passover" was originally published as "Passover. Kyiv. 1995" in Issue 6 (2018) of *Eastern Iowa Review* and chosen for their "Best Lyric Prose Plus" published in 2019.

"Kyivsky Waltz" lyrics by Andriy Malyshko.

Olga Golovko is a superstar for reading my garbled bits of Ukrainian and Russian and making them make sense. Any mistakes are mine, not hers.

Thanks to the wonderful people at Razom for their dedication and much needed efforts. Together we are Ukraine.

And thanks to you, the reader, for buying this book.

All of the author's proceeds from this publication will be donated to Razom, an NGO dedicated to providing humanitarian aid to Ukraine. For more information, go to https://www.razomforukraine.org/

This book is set in Kabel and Fermata, a new typeface created by Taimur Hyat.

Publisher: Leah Huete de Maines
Editor: Christen Kincaid
Cover Art: KS Lack. Under the Banner of Lenin (Revised)
Author Photo: Thomas Gallagher and Konrad Will
Cover Design: Elizabeth Maines McCleavy

Order online. www.finishinglinepress.com
also available on amazon.com

Author inquiries and mail orders:
Finishing Line Press
PO Box 1626
Georgetown, Kentucky 40324
USA

Table of Contents

The first 72 hours: September 1994

Chkalova Street 1

Old New Year 3

Volodymyrs'kyy Rynok | Volodymyr Market 4

you 6

Kashtan | Chestnut 7

Notes from a Passover 8

Victory Day 10

Sonyashnyk | Sunflower 11

Kyiv Then to Now 12

Hydropark 14

Dzerkalo | The Mirror 16

Yom Kippur 18

On the Dnipro 19

northport new york 20

Oblipykha | Sea buckthorn 22

Druzhby Narodiv Boulevard 23

Ne Nashi | The Other 24

The last 72 hours: September 1996

Можете ли вы её спросить, где находятся шнуры для компьютеров? Она не знает, или она no understand? Попробуйте использовать слова попроще. Боже мой она даже не может сказать «хорошо». Что мы будем с ней делать? Ми намагалися розмовляти з нею українською? Боже це ще гірше. Главное — тримаємося російської мови. Вона нам нужна, щоби работать. Она ничего не понимает. Мы знаем кого-нибудь, кто может с ней поговорить? О чём они думают, когда отправляют её сюда? Она не может даже проехаться в метро самостоятельно, нам придётся её повсюду возить. И не смотря на то, как улыбается! Она уже ніколи не буде счастлива, так почему она улыбается? Она ничего no understand — нічого. Посмотри на неё? Все глаза. О чём она думает? Кто-нибудь знает, как спросить ее об этом на английском языке? Боже мой, что мы будем делать? Она nothing…

Could she speak Russian or Ukrainian? Why did I think I could… blacklisting themselves in order to have jobs. Imagine being so brave to leave home. Talk to someone but all I can do is say ya ne ponimayu, I do not understand. Ponimayu, ya ne ponimayu. I have so much I wish to say. I feel so lost and alone. I have to be thinking about firing me. I would be free to speak uncensored. These people have given up their jobs. It's all just noise. I am useless. No one speaks English—why would they? I see their mouths moving and understand nothing. What a disaster. No newspaper, to finally be…

The first 72 hours: September 1994

Chkalova Street

The car belongs to my boss
Vladimir Pavlovich the Editor
in Chief. His driver (whose
name I was told but lost) is a
thick-necked hulk little older
than me with oil under his nails
and green-black tattoos on his
fingers. He says something
words flutter by but I cannot
catch them. This is not how the
émigrés spoke over extra-credit teas
voices swelling into small symphonies
of languid disillusion—*always
remember to use the formal, my dear, when
addressing your elders*—here everyone
speaks in rumbling bursts, gulping
words down before they end and
swallowing my comprehension along
with them. The driver turns down a
cobblestone street and stops and I
realize I must live here and get out.
I am starving. All I had to eat today
was bread salvaged from sandwiches.
Everyone here eats meat; that I cannot
since I've been ill makes no sense in
any language. I go back outside. The
stores are closed (not that I would
brave them) but there is a kiosk whose
light beckons from the encroaching
darkness. A few people mull about. I
feel them watching—clothes, walk
me: nothing fits. I start a smile. Stop.

That isn't done here. I point without
speaking. Two thousand seven hundred
post-communist monopoly notes
buy a bag of chips without the
chicken on them, what I hope are
some cookies and a bottle of wine.
None of this seems real. It is hard
not to run as I walk away.
The apartment's pink wallpaper
and red tassel curtains make me feel
like I'm Jonah inside his whale. An
old phone hangs on the wall next
to a radio with three channels
and no off button. I pick up the
receiver though there is no one to
call. Voices float up the line. A burst
of static sounds like laughter. I hang
up and then cut my hand trying
to open the wine bottle. Drops of
wine and blood mingle on the plastic
countertop, a Rorschach in red. I look
for a pattern that makes sense but
there's nothing to see except a
mess of my own making.

Old New Year

Endlessly falling
snow, with the weight of Trotsky
warm upon my lap
salvation found caring for
this small, half-mad orange cat

Volodymyrs'kyy Rynok | Volodymyr Market

Poprobuytye! Poprobuyte!
Women, faces ruddy, chapped
half-hidden within layers of
damp wool, sit behind rows
of once-identical tin containers
made unique by age and care.
Poprobuytye! Poprobuyte!
On a mezzanine draped in a
miasma of stale breath and
cigarette smoke, people swarm
around me, moving in patterns
I cannot comprehend.
Poprobuytye! Nuzno poprobovat'!
A hand snares my wrist and pulls
me close. I wait, hips pressed
against cold metal, for the push
of the crowd

none comes.
Poprobuytye, poprobuytye—
words slower as she gently pulls
off my glove and twists my arm
a fortune teller in reverse. Her
spoon dollops thick cream
        stinging, wet, vaguely unctuous
onto the back of my hand.
Try it, try it, she urges.

No one looks (though everyone
sees) my tentative taste. Flavors
flood my mouth
      cut-grass icicles
      the tang of a morning's kiss
      mushrooms misted with earth
greedily I turn cat and lick my
paw clean. Metal-laced teeth
flash in laughter.
Try mine! Try mine! the next woman
calls and down the line I dance—
all of us happy to share back
when foreign was new.

you

    walk into the party
    hours late
    a clichéd mix-tape
    of my greatest hits
        floppy dark hair
          bluegreen eyes
            cheekbones as sharp
        as the chip on your shoulder
    in second-hand dickies
    and a mustard yellow
    ski sweater so awful
    it had to be ironic
    they said you were
    a musician masquerading
    as an english teacher
    fluent in russian
    (you even read
    my mirror)
    interesting and sweet and
    best of all
    transient
    you were going home
    no matter what
            no matter whom
    come june

    perfect

Kashtan | Chestnut

A playful wind twirls
blossoms into a raucous
revel, suffusing
the air in spring's heady scent—
freedom is an opening

Notes from a Passover

Here, in the city of Pechersk and Babyn Yar, I expected my celebration to be a quiet affair. How was I to know that most of my colleagues had Jewish branches hidden in their family trees?

The fax machine beeps again. The wealth of my loved ones—nurtured though continents and centuries, passed faithfully from mouth to ear—spills forth in an endless scroll of perforated paper. Food is a sermon everyone understands.

Their stares are a silence that shouts. *Not here—around the corner—stop asking!* a voice chastises from within the passing crowd. I turn to find a section of market I've never seen. Nearby sit a father and son in clean but blood-stained butcher smocks. I ask my carefully prepared question once more: *Do you have a shank bone, from a lamb? Yes*, they reply. *Happy Passover.*

The Rabbi motions me to sit without offering to shake my hand. Our religion shares the same name but the gulf dividing our beliefs is too wide to cross. Then we realize we are both Americans from New York City and Yankee fans. I leave the synagogue lugging enough matzo to feed me for a month.

Such bad luck, to borrow an egg, my neighbor huffs fondly. *Wait until the stores open tomorrow.* When I tell her why I need the egg, her goodwill crumples up and blows away. *Ty Zhydivka?* she hisses. I flinch. This word, from the woman who invites me in for tea, whose daughter I help with her homework? *Nyet. Ya Yevreyka.* I am a Jew, not a Yid.

Horror finds a home between us. *Is one egg really that important?* she asks. I think about what the egg represents: Life. Sacrifice. Potential. My Seder would be meaningless without its. *Da,* I say. It is. She nods slowly and turns away, but comes back with one egg. *Keep it,* she whispers. *Don't ever tell of this to my husban*d. She never speaks to me again.

Guests arrive; the apartment grows but cannot fit inside itself. We take the front door off to use as a table. Still people keep crowding in. Languages fill the air, dancing together in a swirl of cigarette smoke. We sing our praises and the thread binding us together thrums. These prayers have been spoken here before; they will be said again when I am gone. The door is open. Elijah, come home.

Victory Day

We tumble out of the apartment
onto the train and set off before
belief settles in

Wrapped around one another we read
and dream as the train lumbers along
rolling by small dusty platforms as

Babushkas cry their wares to our
windows, slip back into darkness
disappear

Morning smells like home; I laugh to kiss
the salt from your lips. Around us bloom
lilacs hued darkest dawn to palest dusk

We walk along streets hungover from days
of glamour, their once grand easter-egg
facades faded and worn

Chance leads us to Potemkin's Steps, striding
down mountains to greet the sea. The harbor
teems with ships reaching towards the horizon

Odesa's clocks strike noon and a cacophony
of sirens bellow in reply. The ground shakes
The sky explodes in a kaleidoscope of sound

Joy pours from my mouth, washing
the world in blue. This is what it
means to love you

Sonyashnyk | Sunflower

The sunflower turns
its face each day, yearning for
what it can never
have. Held fast by earth's embrace
dreaming of the sun's last kiss

Hydropark

1

The metro settles in its tracks and
we disembark amid the gaggle onto
a hurdy-gurdy island where too-thin
girls in thigh-high skirts flirt at drunks
propping up crumbling walls

We walk through a wood scarred by
badly poured concrete and broken glass
too grimy to glitter, then weeds part
revealing a miracle—a sagging dock
moored by rowboats

From the water Kyiv lies transformed
brutal buildings soften when bathed
in dappled sunshine; the silver robes of
Rodina-Mat' glow in surprising concert
with Lavra's golden domes

Basking on concrete beaches
strangers laugh and wave as we glide
pass, their hooded eyes and grim
mouths shed like old skins. You smile
offering me one last gift

2

the music drew us
a sound from a
different age

following we found
a tattered pavilion
empty except for a few

pensioners, waltzing
round and round
they danced

invoking a memory
from a story
we could not share

                3

After you left I would ride the metro
to the island, waiting as the water
loomed closer like a bruise emerging
from under my skin

Each time I told myself I would get off
walk the paths we took, watch others
row and laugh and swim. Build new
memories. New dreams

The doors would open. Close. I stayed
stuck in my seat, craning my neck for one
last glimpse of sunshine before the tunnel
swallowed us from view

Dzerkalo | The Mirror

Birth of The Mirror
She stole in on borrowed feet. We left her in darkness, ink still wet on her skin, her soul wrapping ribbons of words around us, marking us as hers. How could something so fragile be so dangerous?

The Mirror Learns Color
White was what she was, new-white snow-white, a promise as pure as the chestnut trees in bloom. Nothing here stays white for long. What is pristine turns

yellow like the fingertips of the worn-torn men who smoked cigarette after cigarette as they schemed and hid their thoughts from view. It is the color she aspires to be: to age; be savored and saved. If not that, then let her rot and return as something

green, rising from the dirt. A mountain of *kupony* provides no more nutrients than dust in the air, but give her greenbacks and see what they grow. Careful though: green-hued too is envy and fear; watch how you go lest it curdles

blue-black like the bruises on her boys—not everyone loves a critic like she does. Caught bought they tried to shred her up stuff her words into their mouths but they could never swallow her all, her boys were too fast for that even though they bled

red like Iuliia's nails, tapping at the keyboard, each word a slash tearing into the fabric of this country that is now and the vastness that was, that echoes in every silence: red red red red red

The Mirror Learns Longing
Sneaking in under the rattle of ill-fitting windows it twines, a heady softness, full of the smell of scalded milk-soaked poppy seeds. The taste in her mouth of fresh yeast. A suggestion of sweetness brushing against her lips...

The Mirror Celebrates
The women spend all afternoon dressing her up. Bottles appear from the air—champagne, vodka, beer. Plates piled high with fresh bread and homemade pickles, lashings of cheese and meat. Pennies would be pinched from somewhere else; scandals and threats could wait. First toast for the day, be it past saint or present sinner. Second for all the women, from now to before. And the third, always for her—our Mirror. The reason why we are here, why we laugh and drink and sing as we wonder what happens next now that the abyss has come and gone.

What a terrible burden to place on one so young. So, laughing, she drinks.

Yom Kippur

Your voice on the phone
overwhelms me. You say *I'm
back* and I want you
to hurt but faith makes me pause

atonement does not mean peace

On the Dnipro

Late September and the *rynok* brims with
an abundance of possibilities
I choose ingredients with wonton care
letting my senses guide me—plump beans, fresh
white onions, tomatoes glowing black-red—
when my bags are full I head underground
surfing along with the metro masses
stop off at the kiosk, get *chipsy* and
chat; add a bottle of Bull's Blood to sip
while chopping and wailing along with my
cat and my tunes. Then a knock on the door
You. Unexpected and armed with more Blood
My evening ends in sorrow and tears, whose
late-night addition to the casserole
made it fantastic.
                              At least that's what
my girlfriends tell me at the Mirror's fall
picnic, drinking beers in the sun as the
Dnipro slow-rolls on by: that tears are the
secret ingredient to many of
life's great meals. Next to us Pavlovich
tends the grill, voice booming, vodka in hand
as Andrei and Sasha circle back for
a third helping. Everyone laughs, happy
I take a sip of beer but all I taste
is the bitter truth buried in their words
About tears shed at night, alone in the
kitchen, long after the men have gone

northport new york

i miss the sound of my
old clock. the flip of each
leaf a heartbeat

kept me sane during the
endless hours of my
teenage years. this

new doppelgänger mocks
me with its silence
i count hours

that are minutes. its red
digital glow never
seems to change. i

miss you. you are where the
sun has fled to, so far
away east. on

a train. traveling through
another brutally
cold day. its chill

burrows into my heart
i trust you, i do, but
my trust is a

fragile thing. no match for
this night when even the
clocks have stopped

pain and i are cellmates
hurting like this is new
you wanted to

go back—see those you loved
before you loved me. how
could i say no?

i want your happiness
to have everyone see
you are happy

and know it's due to me
i trust you, i do, but
her? not so much

i slip downstairs. twine the
phone cord around my wrist
a spiral noose

do not cry do not cry
the line clicks and clicks
so many steps

needed to reach you. i
will let the phone ring on
and on. hear the

silence that surrounds it
let that be my lesson

then you answer

Oblipykha | Sea buckthorn

Caressed by seas' tears
you endure where others fail
silver to silver
we touch, reflecting love more
vibrant than the setting sun

Druzhby Narodiv Boulevard

Bordello-red tassels hiding cotton
Candy walls, playing at being grown-up
Hearing time clip by over cobblestones
Nestled tight within puzzle-box courtyards
Looking out from everything I wanted
Watching my picture of paradise peel
Now there's a vista of abandoned cars
Dripping rust on weeds in a torn-up lot
The highway rumbles from nighttime passage
Of army trucks with painted-over names
The air tastes tired and shabby and old
But here nothing is yours or mine—just ours
They say that tree outside our window is
An apricot and will bear fruit, come spring

Ne Nashi | The Other

My life here is like a string of amber
beads: transformed by pressure into something

precious, valued for its imperfections
I devised this trip to show her the world

we share, perfect as life so rarely is
didn't see that meant perfect-for-me (a

bathtub in the kitchen!) not until we
stood for an hour waiting for our long-

distance call to connect and she entered
the stall—trapped in a confessional of

the Soviet kind, where everyone can
judge your sins. Even turned away from me

I know what it looks like
when my mother cries

There's no déjà vu that inoculates
my father and me and gives us a pass

of sorts. Colors here do not sing to her
everything is off-key. A cross is not

hers if it has extra beams. She is not
some other that used come from here. She

is just foreign, so she sees what I no
longer do: the crumbling concrete. Water

that can't be drunk. Rows of empty stalls where
there used to be food. A hard place full of

people with few choices, living the best
lives they can. A daughter who has denied

half of what she is to make herself fit
No wonder she's crying all alone in

a phone box to my father thousands of
miles away. How can I blame her for

taking my gift of amber and seeing
only the fly, forever stuck in sap?

She knows why I would find such hardship
seductive. She knows how badly I'm cracked

How to show I've changed? Living no longer
feels like a burden endured for others

I will reach under the green-velvet leaves
of an old fig tree and taste its ripe fruit

lie down on a beach to feel how rocks kissed
by the sun warm my skin. I love this place

It brought me home
It brought me you

But now, watching my mother cry, I think
it's time for us to go

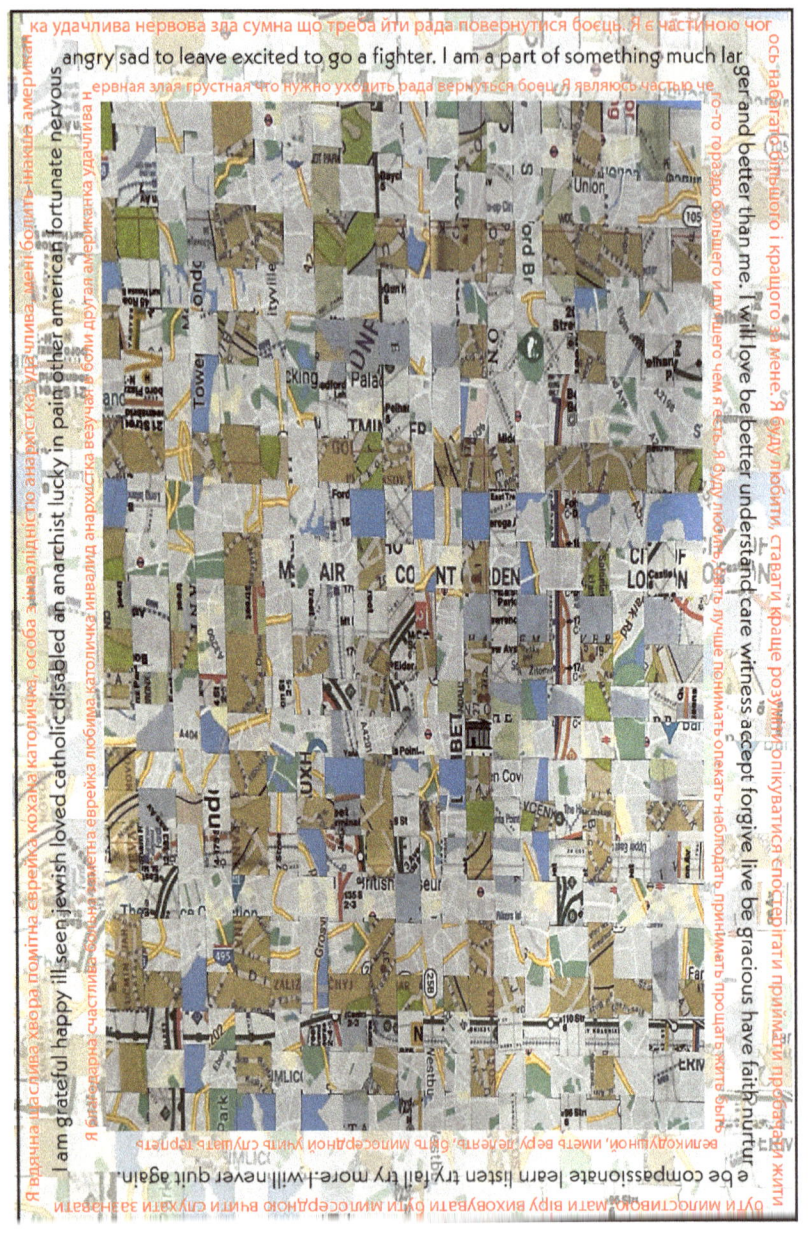

The last 72 hours: September 1996

www.ingramcontent.com/pod-product-compliance
Lightning Source LLC
Chambersburg PA
CBHW040308170426
43194CB00022B/2947